# Essential English
## : Begin Again

**Key Features**
- Picture Description
- Grammatical Expressions
- Let's Talk Dialogue Practice
- Check It Out Interactive Activities
- One Step Ahead Review Tasks

MP3

**CARROT HOUSE**

**CARROT HOUSE**
P.O.Box #2924, St. Marys, Ontario, Canada

**Essential English : Begin Again**
© Carrot House

All rights reserved. No part of this publication may be reproduced, stored in a retrieval system, or transmitted in any form or by any means without the prior permission in writing of Carrot House

**Printed** : June 2022

**Author** : Carrot Language Lab

**ISBN** 978-89-6732-179-6

**Carrot Global Inc.**
3F, 268-20, Itaewon-ro, Hannamdong, Yongsan-gu, Seoul, 04399, South Korea

# Curriculum Map

CARROT

| Course | Level 1 | Level 2 | Level 3 | Level 4 | Level 5 | Level 6 | Level 7 | Text Book |
|---|---|---|---|---|---|---|---|---|
| **General Conversation** | Essential English : Begin Again / Pre Get Up to Speed 1~2 / Daily Focused English 1 | New Get Up to Speed+ 1~2 / Daily Focused English 2 | New Get Up to Speed+ 1~2 / New Get Up to Speed+ 3~4 | New Get Up to Speed+ 3~4 / New Get Up to Speed+ 5~6 | New Get Up to Speed+ 5~6 / New Get Up to Speed+ 7~8 | New Get Up to Speed+ 7~8 | | |
| **Discussion** | | | Active Discussion 1 | Active Discussion 1 / Chicken Soup Course | Active Discussion 2 / Chicken Soup Course / Dynamic Information & Digital Technology | Dynamic Discussion / Chicken Soup Course / Dynamic Information & Digital Technology | Dynamic Discussion / Dynamic Information & Digital Technology | |
| **Business Conversation** | Pre Business Basics 1 | Pre Business Basics 1 / Pre Business Basics 2 | Pre Business Basics 2 / Business Basics 1 | Business Basics 1 / Business Basics 2 | Business Basics 2 / Business Practice 1 | Business Practice 1 / Business Practice 2 | Business Practice 2 | |
| **Global Biz Workshop** | | | | Effective Business Writing Skills (Workbook) / Effective Presentation Skills (Workbook) | Effective Business Writing Skills (Workbook) / Effective Presentation Skills (Workbook) / Effective Negotiation Skills (Workbook) / Cross-Cultural Training 1~2 (Workbook) / Leadership Training Course (Workbook) | Effective Negotiation Skills (Workbook) / Cross-Cultural Training 1~2 (Workbook) / Leadership Training Course (Workbook) | | |
| **Business Skills** | | | Simple & Clear Technical Writing Skills | Simple & Clear Technical Writing Skills / Effective Business Writing Skills / Effective Meeting Skills / Business Communication (Negotiation) / Effective Presentation Skills | Effective Business Writing Skills / Effective Meeting Skills / Business Communication (Negotiation) / Effective Presentation Skills / Marketing 1 | Marketing 1 / Marketing 2 / Management | Marketing 2 / Management | |
| **On the Job English** | | | Construction English in Use 1~4 / Public Service English in Use | Human Resources / Accounting and Finance / Marketing and Sales / Production Management / Automotive / Banking and Commerce / Medical and Medicine / Information Technology / Construction / Construction English in Use 1~4 / Public Service English in Use | Human Resources / Accounting and Finance / Marketing and Sales / Production Management / Automotive / Banking and Commerce / Medical and Medicine / Information Technology / Construction | | | |

※ This Curriculum Map illustrates the entire line-up of textbooks at CARROT HOUSE.

# Essential English
## : Begin Again

## Introduction

### Carrot House Methodology
*Andragogical Approach & Productive English*

The teaching of children (pedagogy) and adult learning (andragogy) are distinctively different. Pedagogy is akin to training and encourages convergent thinking and rote learning. It is compulsory, centered on the teacher and the imparting of information with minimal control by the learner. Andragogy, by contrast, is about education as freedom. It encourages divergent thinking and active learning. It is voluntary, learner oriented, and opens up vistas for continuing learning. Adults need to feel independent and in control of their learning. Therefore, Carrot House curriculum is based on andragogy and is designed to encourage learners' participation and engagement by providing more task-based activities and opportunities to frequently interact in the classroom.

People want to achieve communicative competence when they learn other languages. English education in EFL environments has been rather focused on the receptive skills of English—listening and reading—which simply increases learners' knowledge about a language, not the competence of using it. If people are well equipped with productive skills—speaking and writing—they will be competent in English communication.

This is why Carrot House curriculum is designed to enhance learners' productive skills throughout the course. This andragogical approach of the Carrot House Curriculum, which focuses on productive English, will enable learners to achieve communication skills necessary for global competence. Carrot House's teaching philosophy and curriculum combine to provide a "Language for Success" for all learners.

### Communicative Language Learning (CLL)

This communicative interaction, the essential component of language acquisition, does not occur in a typical, non-meaningful, fun-oriented conversation with native speakers. It occurs in a negotiated interaction through which a well-trained teacher provides the comprehensible input that is appropriate to the learners. The learners, at the same time, actively utilize the opportunities given to them by the teachers.

To this end, the Communicative Language Learning (CLL) method is employed in the field of Foreign Language Acquisition. The CLL method provides activities that are geared toward using language pragmatically, authentically and functionally with the intention of achieving meaningful purposes.

# Course Objective

## Overview

Essential English : Begin Again is designed to improve beginners' proficiency in spoken and written English. This book aims to help beginners' communicate in English with confidence by providing as many opportunities as possible through constant classroom interactions and systematic pattern practices.

## Composition

Essential English: Begin Again consists of sixteen units. Each unit, composed of nine sections, examines two grammatical expressions and pattern practices.

**2. Grammatical Expression I**

Presents the first grammar point of the lesson

**1. Getting Started**

Opens each unit with short warm up activities of describing the image and open discussion

**3. Let's Talk I**

Uses the first grammar point in a short dialogue where a mp3 is also provided. Comprehension questions are also provided to check the learners understanding

**4. Check It Out**

Provides an area for speaking practice using the grammar and language points

### 5. Grammatical Expression II

Presents the second grammar point of the lesson

### 8. One Step Ahead

Reviews the topic through open ended discussion questions and writing tasks

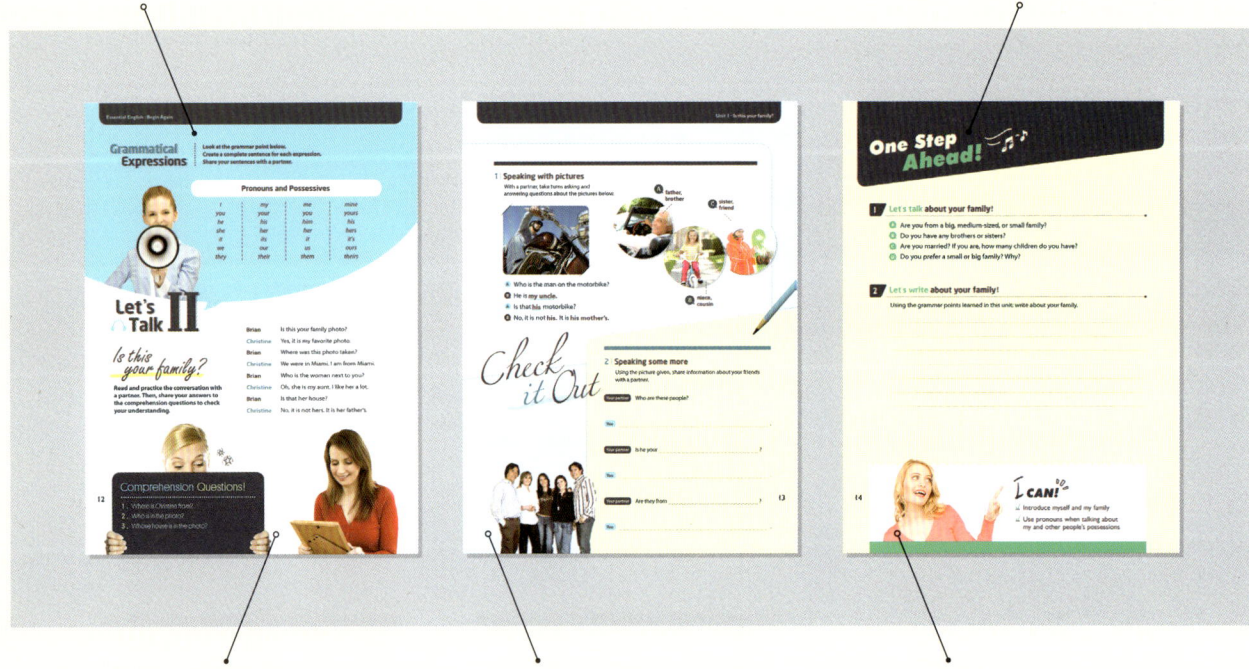

### 6. Let's Talk II

Uses the second grammar point in a short dialogue where a mp3 is also provided. Comprehension questions are also provided to check the learners understanding

### 7. Check It Out

Provides an area for speaking practice using the grammar and language points

### 9. I CAN

Provides an area where the learning objectives of the unit, provided in Getting Started, can be reviewed

# Essential English
## : Begin Again

Essential English : Begin Again

# Contents

| Unit | | Grammar Focus | Speaking Lesson | Key Vocabulary |
|---|---|---|---|---|
| 1 | **Is this your family?** <br> page. 9 | • "be" verb <br> • pronouns <br> • possessive <br> • objectives | • What's your name? <br> • Is this your family? | • family tree <br> • names of countries <br> • personal objects |
| 2 | **What a nice place!** <br> page. 15 | • nouns (singular/plural) <br> • this, that, it <br> • there is/are <br> • have/has | • What a nice apartment! <br> • Is there a nice coffee shop around here? | • rooms at home <br> • house objects <br> • places in towns |
| 3 | **What are you doing?** <br> page. 21 | • present continuous <br> • wh-questions (1) | • Who are they? <br> • What are you doing now? | • clothing and accessories <br> • everyday verbs |
| 4 | **Do you get up early in the morning?** <br> page. 27 | • present tense (1) | • What do you do after work? <br> • What do you usually do on Saturday? | • never / usually / always <br> • everyday verbs |
| 5 | **What do you have for breakfast?** <br> page. 33 | • present tense (2) <br> • wh-questions (2) | • Aren't you hungry? <br> • He sings rock. | • food <br> • entertainment |
| 6 | **What can you do on vacation?** <br> page. 39 | • can for ability <br> • can for possibility | • I can speak English. <br> • You can do a million things. | • verbs for job ability <br> • sightseeing |
| 7 | **How was your trip to Florida?** <br> page. 45 | • past tense (1) & be verb <br> • questions | • I was born in Seoul. <br> • How was your trip to Florida? | • adjectives to describe things and feelings <br> • verbs for ability |
| 8 | **What did you do last night?** <br> page. 51 | • past tense (2) | • What did you do last night? <br> • How was your weekend? | • past verbs for activities <br> • time expressions for the past |

# Contents

| Unit | Grammar Focus | Speaking Lesson | Key Vocabulary |
|---|---|---|---|
| 9  **What are you going to do?**  *page. 57* | · future with "will"  · future with "be going to" | · What are you going to get her?  · What are you going to do tonight? | · special days  · special occasions |
| 10  **Would you like to go out for dinner?**  *page. 63* | · present continuous for future | · Would you like to come with me?  · I have to make some food for a Christmas party. | · verbs for invitation  · suggestions  · expressions to turn down an invitation |
| 11  **He's very attractive.**  *page. 69* | · be + adjective  · a(n) + adjective + noun | · She is kind of cute.  · He has curly brown hair. | · adjectives for appearance  · color |
| 12  **It is fantastic.**  *page. 75* | · be + adjective  · be + not + adjective  · be-questions | · It was awful.  · You have to know life is not easy. | · adjectives for feeling  · adjectives for personality |
| 13  **I think I am lost.**  *page. 81* | · preposition for location  · how to verb | · Is there an Internet cafe near here?  · Excuse me. I think I am lost. | · expressions for giving directions  · places around town |
| 14  **Would you care for some dessert?**  *page. 87* | · countable/ uncountable nouns  · a little vs. a few  · some vs. any | · What do you want for dinner?  · I am watching my weight. | · vegetables / fruits / drinks  · expressions for offering things |
| 15  **Do you mind if I use your car?**  *page. 93* | · modals for requests  · modals for getting a permission | · Could you tell him to call me later?  · Do you mind if I use your car tonight? | · expressions on the phone  · expressions for asking opinions |
| 16  **Wasn't it a little scary?**  *page. 99* | · tag questions  · negative questions | · I can't have my lunch, can I?  · Wasn't it a little scary? | · Be-verb review  · Do-verb review |

Unit 1

# Is this your family?

## 1

### Learning Objectives

**After completing this unit, you should be able to...**

+ Introduce yourself and your family
+ Use pronouns when talking about your and others' possessions

### Getting Started

**Answer the questions about the picture above.**

1. Is this a small or a large family?
2. How many members are there in this family?
3. Where are they?

Essential English : Begin Again

## Grammatical Expressions

Look at the grammar point below.
Read and create complete sentences using the words given.
Share your sentences with a partner.

### "Be" verbs (Present)

| I am … | I am not … | Am I …? |
| You are … | You are not … | Are you …? |
| He / She / It is … | He / She / It is not … | Is he / she / it …? |
| We are … | We are not … | Are we …? |
| They are … | They are not … | Are they …? |

## Let's Talk I

### What's your name?

Read and practice the conversation with a partner. Then, share your answers to the comprehension questions to check your understanding.

**James**  Hello. My name is James. What's your name?

**Jessica**  Hi. I'm Jessica. Nice to meet you.

**James**  Nice to meet you, too.
Are you from America?

**Jessica**  Yes, I am. I am from New York.
How about you?
Where are you from?

**James**  I am from Seoul, Korea.

**Jessica**  Really? My husband is from Korea, too.

### Comprehension Questions!

1. Who is having this conversation?
2. Where is Jessica from?
3. Where is her husband from?

Unit 1 · Is this your family?

## 1 | Speaking with pictures

With a partner, take turns asking and answering questions about the pictures below.

A Mary, South Africa
C Stanley, Taiwan
B Jonas, Sweden

**A** Who is that?
**B** That is **Harry.**
**A** Where is he from?
**B** He is from **New Zealand.**

## 2 | Speaking some more

Share information about yourself with a partner.

**Your partner** What's your name?

**You** ................................................................. .

**Your partner** Are you from ................................................. ?

**You** .................................................................
I am from ................................................. .

**Your partner** Is your husband / wife / boyfriend / girlfriend
from ................................................. , too?

**You** ................................................................. .

11

Essential English : Begin Again

## Grammatical Expressions

Look at the grammar point below.
Create a complete sentence for each expression.
Share your sentences with a partner.

### Pronouns and Possessives

| | | | |
|---|---|---|---|
| I | my | me | mine |
| you | your | you | yours |
| he | his | him | his |
| she | her | her | hers |
| it | its | it | it's |
| we | our | us | ours |
| they | their | them | theirs |

## Let's Talk II

### Is this your family?

Read and practice the conversation with a partner. Then, share your answers to the comprehension questions to check your understanding.

**Brian**    Is this your family photo?

**Christine**    Yes, it is my favorite photo.

**Brian**    Where was this photo taken?

**Christine**    We were in Miami. I am from Miami.

**Brian**    Who is the woman next to you?

**Christine**    Oh, she is my aunt. I like her a lot.

**Brian**    Is that her house?

**Christine**    No, it is not hers. It is her father's.

### Comprehension Questions!

1. Where is Christine from?
2. Who is in the photo?
3. Whose house is in the photo?

Unit 1 · Is this your family?

## 1 | Speaking with pictures

With a partner, take turns asking and answering questions about the pictures below.

A father, brother
C sister, friend
B niece, cousin

A Who is the man on the motorbike?
B He is **my uncle.**
A Is that **his** motorbike?
B No, it is not **his.** It is **his mother's.**

# Check it Out

## 2 | Speaking some more

Using the picture given, share information about your friends with a partner.

**Your partner** Who are these people?

**You** ................................................................................................ .

**Your partner** Is he your ............................................................................ ?

**You** ................................................................................................ .

**Your partner** Are they from ...................................................................... ?

13

**You** ................................................................................................ .

# One Step Ahead!

**1. Let's talk about your family!**

- A. Are you from a big, medium-sized, or small family?
- B. Do you have any brothers or sisters?
- C. Are you married? If you are, how many children do you have?
- D. Do you prefer a small or big family? Why?

**2. Let's write about your family!**

Using the grammar points learned in this unit; write about your family.

## I CAN!

✓ Introduce myself and my family

✓ Use pronouns when talking about my and other people's possessions

Unit 2

# What a nice place!

## 2

### Learning Objectives

After completing this unit, you should be able to...

+ Talk about your home and your neighborhood
+ Use "have" to talk about possessions

### Getting Started

Answer the questions about the pictures above.

1. What's happening in the small photo? Where are they?
2. What do you see in the big photo?
3. Are the images similar to your city?

Essential English : Begin Again

## Grammatical Expressions

Look at the grammar point below.
Create complete sentences for each of the phrases given below.
Share your sentences with a partner.

**VERB : have (present simple)**

| I have … | I don't have … | Do I have …? |
| You have … | You don't have … | Do you have …? |
| He/She/It has … | He/She/It doesn't have … | Does he/she/it have …? |
| We have … | We don't have … | Do we have …? |
| They have … | They don't have … | Do they have …? |

## Let's Talk 1

### What a nice apartment!

Read and practice the conversation with a partner. Then, share your answers to the comprehension questions to check your understanding.

**Mark**    Wow, you have a nice apartment.

**Hillary**    Thanks. It's not bad. This is the kitchen.

**Mark**    It's really nice. Does it have a dishwasher?

**Hillary**    No, it doesn't. But there is a big cabinet and a new refrigerator.

**Mark**    That's good. Do you have a microwave?

**Hillary**    No, but I think I need to buy one. Do you have one?

**Mark**    Yes, I do. It is very convenient.

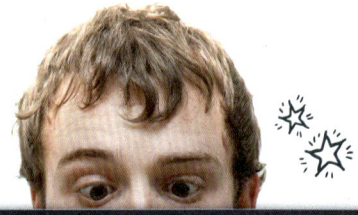

### Comprehension Questions!

1. In what room does this conversation take place?
2. What does the apartment have?
3. What does Hillary need to buy?

Unit 2 · What a nice place!

## 1 | Speaking with pictures

With a partner, take turns asking and answering questions about the pictures below.

A  library, living room, television

C  dining room, kitchen, table

B  balcony, bedroom, bookshelf

**A** He has a nice house. Does he have **a yard?**
**B** No, he doesn't. But he has **a big balcony.**
**A** Does **the balcony** have **a bench?**
**B** No, but I think he needs one.

*Check it Out*

## 2 | Speaking some more

Using the picture given, share information about the area with a partner.

**Your partner**  This is a nice place. Do you have a _____?

**You**  Yes, I do. And there is a _____
and _____.

**Your partner**  That's good. Does the room have a
_____?

**You**  _____. But I think I need one.
Do you have a _____?

**Your partner**  Yes, I do. It is very convenient.

17

Essential English : Begin Again

# Grammatical Expressions

Look at the grammar point below.
Read the information given and answer the questions below.

### There is / are

| There is a television. | There is not a television. | Is there a television? |
| There are some books. | There are not any books. | Are there any books? |

* Which sentences are singular?
  Which sentences are plural?
* What verb is used for plural sentences?

## Let's Talk II

### Is there a nice coffee shop around here?

Read and practice the conversation with a partner. Then, share your answers to the comprehension questions to check your understanding.

| Sean | I love this neighborhood. |
| Katie | Me too. I'd like some coffee. |
| | Is there a nice coffee shop around here? |
| Sean | Yes, there is one just around the corner. |
| Katie | Is it expensive? |
| Sean | No, not at all. |
| | And their coffee is really wonderful. |
| Katie | After that, I need to go to the book store. |
| Sean | There is a big book store near the coffee shop. |
| Katie | Oh, sounds good. |

### Comprehension Questions!

1. Where is the coffee shop?
2. How does their coffee taste?
3. Where are they going after having coffee?

Unit 2 · What a nice place!

## 1 | Speaking with pictures

With a partner, take turns asking and answering questions about the pictures below.

**A** fast food restaurant, bank

**C** movie theater, park

**B** supermarket, pharmacy

**A** I'd like some bread. Are there any **bakeries** around here?

**B** Yes, there is one just around the corner.

**A** And I also want to go to **the post office.**

**B** There is **a post office** near **the bakery.**

**A** That sounds good.

*Check it Out*

## 2 | Speaking some more

Using information about your area, share with your partner about your neighborhood.

**Your partner** I'm hungry. Are there any restaurants around here?

**You** Yes, ................................................................. .

**Your partner** And after that I'd like some coffee.

**You** There are some ................................................. .

**Your partner** Are they expensive?

**You** No, ................................................................. .

# One Step Ahead!

## 1 Let's talk about your town!

**A** Do you have a favorite restaurant near your home?
**B** How often do you go there?
**C** Is it expensive?

## 2 Let's write about your house!

Using the grammar points learned in this chapter; write about your house.

_____
_____
_____
_____
_____
_____
_____

# I CAN!

✓ Talk about my home and my neighborhood
✓ Use "have" to talk about possessions

# Unit 3

# What are you doing?

## 3

### Learning Objectives

**After completing this unit, you should be able to...**

+ Use the present continuous to talk about actions that are now in progress
+ Use proper sentence structure and vocabulary to ask questions

### Getting Started

**Answer the questions about the pictures above.**

1. Who is working on a computer?
2. What are Sue and Janet doing?
3. Is Jane playing the guitar?

Essential English : Begin Again

## Grammatical Expressions

Look at the grammar point below.
Create a complete sentence for each expression.
Share your sentences with a partner.

### Present Continuous

| I am (not) learning … | Am I learning …? | Yes, you are. | What am I doing …? |
| You are studying … | Are you studying …? | Yes, I am. | What are you doing …? |
| He/She/It is running … | Is he/she/it running …? | Yes, he is. | What is he/she/it doing …? |
| We are working … | Are we working …? | Yes, you are. | What are we doing …? |
| They are having .. | Are they having …? | Yes, they are. | What are they doing …? |

* **Grammar Tip :** subject + be + VERB + /ing/
  I + am + STUDY + ing
  **I am studying.**

* **Present Continuous describes :**
  • actions that are taking place at the moment
  • long term actions that are currently in progress
  • plans in the future (i.e. 'going to')

## Let's Talk I

### Who are they?

Read and practice the conversation with a partner. Then, share your answers to the comprehension questions to check your understanding.

**Aaron**    Monica, I don't know anyone at this party.
**Monica**   Don't worry. I will introduce you.
            See that man over there. That is Harry.
**Aaron**    Who is the woman wearing the red dress?
**Monica**   The one drinking a glass of wine?
**Aaron**    Yes, she is wearing black shoes.
**Monica**   Oh, she is Rita, my best friend.
            Her father is very rich.
**Aaron**    Really? Does she have a boyfriend?

### Comprehension Questions!

1. Who does Aaron know at the party?
2. Who is Rita?
3. What is she wearing?

Unit 3 · What are you doing?

## 1 | Speaking with pictures

With a partner, take turns asking and answering questions about the pictures below.

**A** running, riding a bike

**C** swimming, doing yoga

**B** wearing shorts, wearing a suit

**A** Hey, she is so beautiful. Do you know her?
**B** Is she **wearing white sunglasses?**
**A** No, she is **wearing a brown hat.**
**B** Oh, that is Mary, my girlfriend.

*Check it Out*

## 2 | Speaking some more

Using the picture given, share information about your friends with a partner.

**Your partner**  Do you know the woman over there?

**You**  Is she _____ .

**Your partner**  No, she is not. She is _____ .

**You**  Oh, that is Jessie, my _____ .

**Your partner**  She is very cute. Does she have a boyfriend?

**You**  _____ .

Essential English : Begin Again

## Grammatical Expressions

Look at the grammar point below.
Read the information given and create your own answers to each question.

### Questions

| | | |
|---|---|---|
| Are you in Seoul? | No, I am not. | Where are you? |
| Are you busy? | Yes, I am. | Why are you busy? |
| Are you cooking at home? | No, I am not | What are you doing? |
| Is she at the office? | No, she is not. | Where is she? |
| Is she tired? | Yes, she is. | Why is she tired? |
| Is she sleeping? | No, she is not. | What is she doing? |

## Let's Talk II

### What are you doing now?

Read and practice the conversation with a partner. Then, share your answers to the comprehension questions to check your understanding.

| | |
|---|---|
| **Kim** | Hi, Jack. This is Kim. |
| **Jack** | Hi, Kim. Are you calling from home? |
| **Kim** | No, I am not. |
| **Jack** | Where are you then? |
| **Kim** | I am in Miami with my parents. |
| **Jack** | In Miami? Why are you there? |
| **Kim** | I am on vacation. |
| **Jack** | What are you doing now? |
| **Kim** | I am staying at the hotel. |
| | It is raining. |

### Comprehension Questions!

1. Where is Kim?
2. Why is she there?
3. Who is with her?
4. What is she doing?

Unit 3 · What are you doing?

## 1 | Speaking with pictures

With a partner, take turns asking and answering questions about the pictures below.

A  gym, exercising
B  restaurant, having dinner
C  movie theater, watching movies

- **A**  Hello, Jessie. Is Mary at home?
- **B**  No, she is not.
- **A**  Where is she?
- **B**  She is **at the library.**
- **A**  Really? Why is she there?
- **B**  She is **studying**, of course.
- **A**  What are you doing?
- **B**  I am watching TV.

*Check it Out*

## 2 | Speaking some more

Using the picture given, share information about what you are doing with a partner.

**Your partner**  Hi, ............................................. . Are you doing anything now?

**You**  Yes, .................................................................................. .

**Your partner**  Why are you doing that at night?

**You**  Because ............................................................................. .

**Your partner**  Oh, I see.

**You**  What ............................................................................. ?

25

# One Step Ahead!

**1** **Let's talk about you!**

  A. What do you think your best friend is doing now?
  B. Are you learning or studying something now?
  C. Are you reading any books now?

**2** **Let's write about your family and friends!**

Using the grammar points learned in this unit; write about what your family and friends are doing now.

## I CAN!

- Use the present continuous to talk about actions that are now in progress
- Use proper sentence structure and vocabulary to ask questions

# Unit 4

# Do you get up early in the morning?

## 4

### Learning Objectives

After completing this unit, you should be able to...

+ Use the present simple to talk about habits and routines
+ Use adverbs to discuss the frequency of your habits

### Getting Started

Answer the questions about the pictures above.

1. What time do you usually get up on weekdays?
2. Which of the activities above do you do on weekends?
3. How do you go to work?

Essential English : Begin Again

## Grammatical Expressions

Look at the grammar point below.
Create a complete sentence for each expression.
Share your sentences with a partner.

### Present Tense

| | | | |
|---|---|---|---|
| I get up | Do I get up …? | Yes, I do. | No, I don't. |
| You get up … | Do you get up …? | Yes, you do. | No, you don't. |
| He/She/It gets up … | Does he/she/it get up …? | Yes, he/she/it does. | No, he/she/it doesn't. |
| We get up … | Do we get up …? | Yes, we do. | No, we don't. |
| They get up … | Do they get up …? | Yes, they do. | No, they don't. |

\* Present Simple describes :
- habits or routines (*I get up at six o'clock every morning.*)
- things that are always true (*Her hair is blonde.*)
- future actions on a regular schedule (*The flight to Seoul leaves at 4pm.*)

## Let's Talk I

### What do you do after work?

Read and practice the conversation with a partner. Then, share your answers to the comprehension questions to check your understanding.

**Peter**  So, what do you do after work?
Do you go straight home?

**Grace**  Well, usually.
Sometimes I meet a friend for dinner.

**Peter**  Oh, where do you usually go?
Do you go somewhere nice?

**Grace**  Do you know Fabio's Restaurant? It's OK.
The food is good and cheap,
but the service is terrible.

**Peter**  Well, actually, I work there. I'm a server.

**Grace**  Really? Oh, I am sorry.

### Comprehension Questions!

1. What does Grace usually do after work?
2. What does Grace think of Fabio's Restaurant?
3. Where does Peter work?

Unit 4 · Do you get up early in the morning?

## 1 | Speaking with pictures

With a partner, take turns asking and answering questions about the pictures below.

**A** take a class, have dinner
**C** go shopping, do the laundry
**B** go jogging, clean the house

**A** What do you do before work?
**B** **I go to the** gym **and** exercise.
**A** Where do you go after work?
**B** **I go straight home and take care of my cat.**
**A** Oh, you are really busy all day.

*Check it Out*

## 2 | Speaking some more

Share information about yourself with a partner.

**Your partner** What do you usually do in the morning before work?

**You** I usually _____ .

**Your partner** Really? What do you do after work?

**You** _____ .

**Your partner** What time do you usually come back home?

**You** _____ .

29

Essential English : Begin Again

# Grammatical Expressions

Look at the grammar point below.
Read the information and create your own sentences.

| Frequency Adverbs | Possibility |
|---|---|
| I <u>never</u> go to work on Sunday. | 0% |
| I <u>rarely</u> go to work on Saturday. | |
| I <u>sometimes</u> work in the office at night. | |
| I <u>often</u> take a nap in the office. | |
| I <u>usually</u> have lunch in the cafeteria. | |
| I <u>always</u> go to work early in the morning. | 100% |

## Let's Talk II

### What do you usually do on Saturday?

Read and practice the conversation with a partner. Then, share your answers to the comprehension questions to check your understanding.

| | |
|---|---|
| **Jason** | What do you usually do on Saturday? |
| **Lynn** | I usually go for a run in the morning. |
| **Jason** | What about in the afternoon? |
| **Lynn** | In the afternoon I often see a movie. |
| **Jason** | Do you ever play sports on the weekend? |
| **Lynn** | Well, sometimes I play tennis. |
| **Jason** | I love tennis. Why don't we play together sometime? |
| **Lynn** | Sure. That sounds great. |

### Comprehension Questions!

1. What does Lynn like to do on Saturdays?
2. What sport does Jason love?

Unit 4 · Do you get up early in the morning?

## 1 | Speaking with pictures

With a partner, take turns asking and answering questions about the pictures below.

A after work, gym, run, sometimes

C on weekends, home, watch TV, often

B after class, restaurant, work part-time, never

**A** What does your **brother** do **after school**?
**B** He usually **goes to the sports club.**
**A** Oh. What does he do there?
**B** He **plays baseball.**
**A** Does he ever go to the movies?
**B** **No**, he **rarely** has time for that.

*Check it Out*

## 2 | Speaking some more

Share information about yourself with a partner.

**Your partner** What do you usually do on Saturday?

**You** I usually _____ .

**Your partner** Do you ever _____ ?

**You** No, I never do that on Saturday.

**Your partner** Oh, I see. What do you do on Sunday evening?

**You** I usually _____ ,
but I never _____ .

31

# One Step Ahead!

## 1 Let's talk about you!

- **A** Do you always eat breakfast?
- **B** What is the first thing you do in the morning?
- **C** Do you take any lessons or classes before or after work?
- **D** Do you ever go out on Sunday nights?

## 2 Let's write about your typical day!

Using the grammar points learned in this unit; write about your typical daily routine.

## I CAN!

✓ Use the present simple to talk about habits and routines

✓ Use adverbs to discuss the frequency of my habits

Unit 5

# What do you have for breakfast?

## 5

### Learning Objectives

**After completing this unit, you should be able to...**

+ Ask more complex questions using question words + do/does
+ Talk about your preferences and favorites

### Getting Started

**Answer the questions about the picture above.**

1. Where do you think this picture was taken?
2. Do you like going to concerts?
3. When do you go to concerts?

Essential English : Begin Again

# Grammatical Expressions

Look at the grammar point below.
Create complete questions with the expressions.
Share you questions and answers with a partner.

### Present Tense

| | | | |
|---|---|---|---|
| What time | | I | go to work? |
| Where | do | you | usually have lunch? |
| What | | we | do in your free time? |
| When | ___ | they | listen to music? |
| Who | | he | usually go to the movies? |
| How often | does | she | eat out? |
| Why | | it | like Korean food? |

## Let's Talk I

### Aren't you hungry?

Read and practice the conversation with a partner. Then, share your answers to the comprehension questions to check your understanding.

**Jaden**  I am hungry. Aren't you hungry?
**Michelle**  No, I'm not. I ate breakfast.
**Jaden**  What do you usually have for breakfast?
**Michelle**  I always have rice and soup at home.
**Jaden**  I never have breakfast at home.
**Michelle**  Where do you eat?
**Jaden**  I always go to the school cafeteria.
It has nice sandwiches and good coffee.
**Michelle**  Coffee is my favorite drink.
Let's go there and have something.

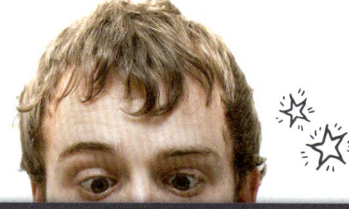

### Comprehension Questions!

1. What does Michelle usually eat for breakfast?
2. Where does Jaden eat breakfast?
3. What is Michelle's favorite drink?

34

Unit 5 · **What do you have for breakfast?**

## 1 | Speaking with pictures

With a partner, take turns asking and answering questions about the pictures below.

**A** breakfast, pancakes and milk

**C** dinner, seafood and beer

**B** lunch, steak and wine

**A** What do you usually have for **breakfast**?

**B** I always have **sandwiches and coffee.**

**A** Do you usually eat at home?

**B** No, I usually **go to** a cafe.

## 2 | Speaking some more

Share information about yourself with a partner.

**Your partner**  Do you have a favorite restaurant for dinner?

**You**  I usually go to ................................................................. .

**Your partner**  What do you have there?

**You**  I ................................................................. .

**Your partner**  How often do you go there?

**You**  ................................................................. .

35

Essential English : Begin Again

## Grammatical Expressions

Look at the grammar point below.
Read and review the information and create your own sentences.
Share your sentences with a partner.

### Present Tense

| I | You/We/They | He/She/It |
|---|---|---|
| am a singer. | are singers. | is a singer. |
| have many fans. | have many fans. | has many fans. |
| sing every day. | sing every day. | sings every day. |
| usually work on Saturday. | usually work on Saturday. | usually works on Saturday. |
| He is my favorite singer. | He is your/our/their favorite singer. | He is his/her favorite singer. |

## Let's Talk II

Read and practice the conversation with a partner. Then, share your answers to the comprehension questions to check your understanding.

**Andrew**   Do you know him?
**Stacey**   No, I don't. Who is he?
**Andrew**   His name is Bon Jovi.
             He is a famous singer in the USA.
**Stacey**   What kind of songs does he sing?
**Andrew**   He sings rock.
             Rock is my favorite style of music.
**Stacey**   I never listen to rock. I like jazz.
             I sometimes go to a jazz bar.
**Andrew**   Jazz bar? That's interesting.

### Comprehension Questions!

1. Who are they talking about?
2. What kind of music does he perform?
3. What is Stacey's favorite style of music?

Unit 5 · What do you have for breakfast?

## 1 | Speaking with pictures

With a partner, take turns asking and answering questions about the pictures below.

**A** TV programs, talk shows, drama

**C** sports, baseball, soccer

**B** movies, horror movies, romantic movies

**A** What kind of **books** do you **read**?
**B** I like **science fiction**. What about you?
**A** I don't **read science fiction**.
    I always **read newspapers**.

## 2 | Speaking some more

Share information about yourself with a partner.

**Your partner** What kind of movies do you like?

**You** ........................................................................... .

**Your partner** Who is your favorite movie star?

**You** ........................................................................... .

**Your partner** How often do you watch a movie?

**You** ........................................................................... .

**Your partner** Who do you usually go with?

**You** ........................................................................... .

# One Step Ahead!

**1  Let's talk about you!**

**A** What is your favorite food?
**B** How often do you eat fast food like hamburgers, pizza and ramen?
**C** What is your favorite web site?
**D** Why do you like that web site?

**2  Let's write about your favorite place!**

Using the grammar points learned in this unit; write about your favorite place to visit with your family or friends.

## I CAN!

✓ Ask more complex questions using question words + do/does

✓ Talk about preferences and favorites

# Unit 6

# What can you do on vacation?

## 6

### Learning Objectives
**After completing this unit, you should be able to...**

+ Discuss your abilities and talents
+ Discuss options and possibilities

### Getting Started
**Answer the questions about the pictures above.**

1. Do you know how to play tennis?
2. Can you play the guitar?
3. What sports or instruments can you play?

Essential English : Begin Again

## Grammatical Expressions

Look at the grammar point below.
Create complete sentences using the expressions.
Share your questions and answers with a partner.

### Can for ability

| I / You / He/She/It / We / They | can swim. | Can | I / You / He/She/It / We / They | swim? | Yes, No, | I / You / He/She/It / We / They | can. can't. |

## Let's Talk I

### I can speak English.

Read and practice the conversation with a partner. Then, share your answers to the comprehension questions to check your understanding.

| Mr. Johns | Hello. Nice to meet you. I'm Mr. Johns. |
| Eileen | Nice to meet you, Mr. Johns. Thanks for offering this job interview. |
| Mr. Johns | First, would you tell me about your skills? |
| Eileen | I can speak English and I am good at business software on the computer. |
| Mr. Johns | That's wonderful. Can you speak Japanese? |
| Eileen | No, I can't. But I am sure I can learn it very quickly. |
| Mr. Johns | OK. What else are you good at? |

### Comprehension Questions!

1. Who is applying for a new job?
2. What language can Eileen speak?
3. What else is she good at?

Unit 6 · What can you do on vacation?

## 1 | Speaking with pictures

With a partner, take turns asking and answering questions about the pictures below.

A Chinese, German
C piano, violin
B lasagna, cookies

A What **sports** can your husband **play**?
B **He** can **swim** well.
A How about you? Can you **swim**, too?
B No, I can't, but I am good at **dancing.**

*Check it Out*

## 2 | Speaking some more

Share information about yourself with a partner.

**Your partner**  Can you tell me about your abilities?
Can you speak ................................................ ?

**You**  ................................................................................ .

**Your partner**  Can you play any sports?

**You**  ................................................................................ .

**Your partner**  Are you good at ................................................ ?

**You**  ................................................................................ .

Essential English : Begin Again

## Grammatical Expressions

Look at the grammar point below.
Read the questions and create your own answers.
Share your answers with a partner.

### Can for possibility

What can I do on a rainy day?
What can you do on holiday?
What can he/she/it do in Seoul?
What can we do on the weekend?
What can they do in Paris?

I / You / He/She/It / We / They can do a million things.

## Let's Talk II

### You can do a million things.

Read and practice the conversation with a partner. Then, share your answers to the comprehension questions to check your understanding.

**Daniel**  Oh, no. It's raining.
How What can we do in New York on a rainy day?

**Sophie**  Oh, come on. We can do a million things.

**Daniel**  Like what?

**Sophie**  We can go to the top of the Empire State Building.

**Daniel**  In this weather?
We can't see anything in the rain.

**Sophie**  Well, you are right. I know. Let's go back to the hotel. We can watch a free movie on TV.

**Daniel**  Yeah. A free movie in the hotel is a great idea.

### Comprehension Questions!

1. What problem are Daniel and Sophie having?
2. Where does Sophie suggest they go?
3. What do they decide to do?

Unit 6 · What can you do on vacation?

## 1 | Speaking with pictures

With a partner, take turns asking and answering questions about the pictures below.

**A** take a ferry, go shopping

**C** eat seafood, watch a show

**B** watch a fashion show, take a bus tour

**A** Finally, we are in **Tokyo.** What can we do here?
**B** First, we can **eat a lot of fresh fish.**
**A** That's good. I really love **fish.** What else can we do?
**B** We can **visit a traditional Japanese museum.**
**A** Can we learn something about **Japanese** culture?
**B** Let's ask the information desk.

*Check it Out*

## 2 | Speaking some more

Share information about a holiday location with a partner.

**Your partner** What can we do in .................................................. ?

**You** We can .................................................. .

**Your partner** I don't like it. What else can we do here?

**You** Well, we can .................................................. .

**Your partner** I don't like it. Can you think of anything more exciting?

**You** Why don't we relax at the hotel?

# One Step Ahead!

## 1. Let's talk about your abilities!

A. Can you name three countries beginning with "C" within one minute?
B. Can you name the capital city of Australia?
C. Are you good at fixing machines?
D. Do you have any special abilities that others don't have?

## 2. Let's write about your skills and talents!

Using the grammar points learned in this unit; write about your skills and talents.

## I CAN!

✓ Discuss my abilities and talents
✓ Discuss options and possibilities

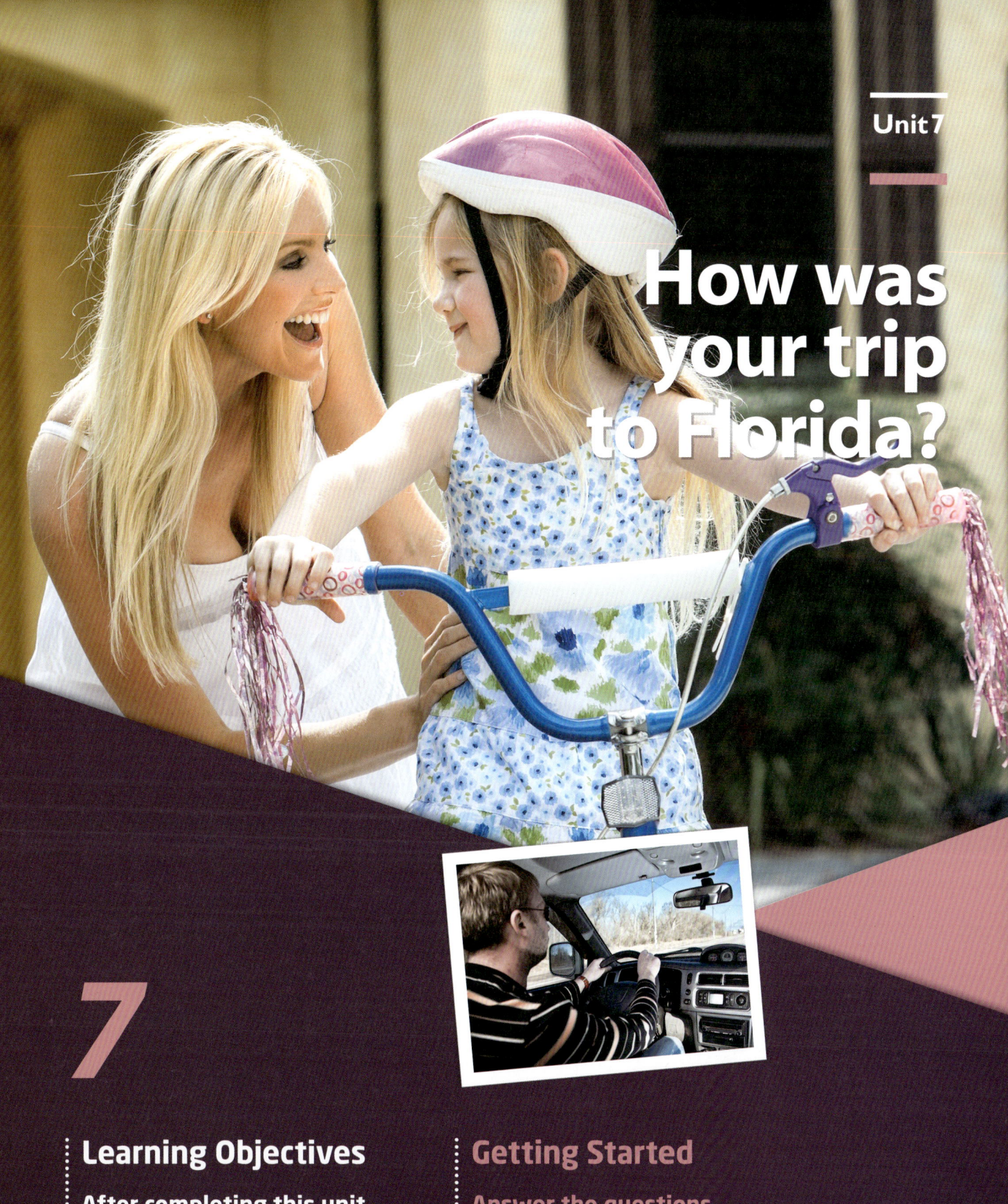

Unit 7

# How was your trip to Florida?

## 7

### Learning Objectives

After completing this unit, you should be able to...

+ Talk about your personal history

### Getting Started

Answer the questions about the pictures above.

1. Can you ride a bike? If you can, how old were you when you learned how to ride a bike?
2. Do you have a driver's license? If yes, when did you get it?
3. Were you a good student in middle school?

Essential English : Begin Again

## Grammatical Expressions

Look at the grammar point below.
Create complete questions with the expressions.
Share your questions and answers with a partner.

### VERB : to be (past simple)

| | | |
|---|---|---|
| I was (not) tired yesterday. | Was I …? | Yes, I was. / No, I wasn't. |
| You were bored last night. | Were you …? | Yes, you were. / No, you weren't. |
| He/She/It was smart. | Was he/she/it …? | Yes, he/she/it was. / No, he/she/it wasn't. |
| We were sad. | Were we …? | Yes, we were. / No, we weren't. |
| They were naughty. | Were they …? | Yes, they were. / No, they weren't. |

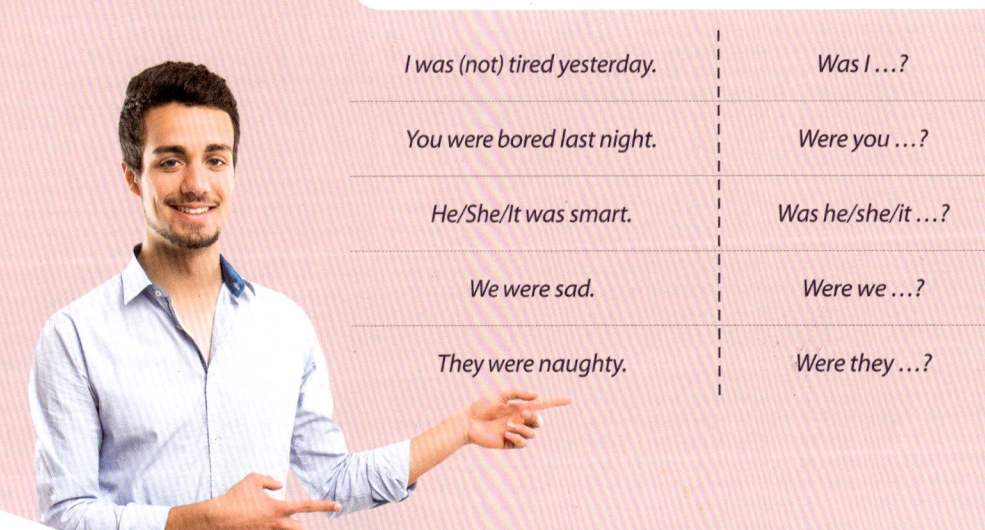

## Let's Talk 1

### I was born in Seoul.

Read and practice the conversation with a partner. Then, share your answers to the comprehension questions to check your understanding.

| | |
|---|---|
| **Amanda** | Who is this boy in the photo? |
| **Paul** | It's me when I was 3 years old. |
| **Amanda** | You were very cute and different from now. |
| **Paul** | Yes. I was very short and thin. |
| **Amanda** | Weren't you born in America? |
| **Paul** | No, I was not. I was born in Seoul. |
| **Amanda** | Could you ride a bike when you were 3? |
| **Paul** | Yeah, I think I was really smart. |

### Comprehension Questions!

1. What age is the boy in the photo?
2. How was he different then?
3. Where was he born?

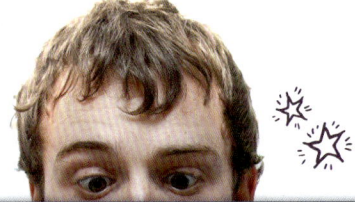

Unit 7 · How was your trip to Florida?

## 1 | Speaking with pictures

With a partner, take turns asking and answering questions about the pictures below.

**A** Austria, 1756, played piano at 3

**C** Germany, 1879, spoke at 8

**B** USA, 1809, lost his mother at 9

**A** Who is the man in this photo?
**B** Don't you know? He is **Picasso**.
**A** Where was he born?
**B** He was born in **Spain in 1881**.
**A** How old was he when he learned to **paint**?
**B** He could **paint when he was 4**.

*Check it Out*

## 2 | Speaking some more

Share information about yourself with a partner.

**Your partner** Were you born in _____?

**You** _____.

**Your partner** Could you play an instrument when you were 10 years old?

**You** _____.

**Your partner** What could you do when you were 8 years old?

**You** I could _____ when I was 8 years old.

**Your partner** Wow, you were very smart.

47

Essential English : Begin Again

## Grammatical Expressions

Look at the grammar point below.
Read the questions and answers, then create your own answers.
Share your answers with a partner.

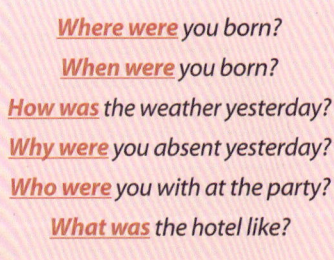

### Questions using BE - past simple

| | |
|---|---|
| **Where were** you born? | I was born in Canada. |
| **When were** you born? | I was born in 1971. |
| **How was** the weather yesterday? | It was sunny. |
| **Why were** you absent yesterday? | I was absent yesterday, because I was sick. |
| **Who were** you with at the party? | I was with my best friend. |
| **What was** the hotel like? | It was fantastic. |

## Let's Talk II

### How was your trip to Florida?

Read and practice the conversation with a partner. Then, share your answers to the comprehension questions to check your understanding.

**Rebecca**   Hi, Joe. How was your trip to Florida?
**Joe**   It was fantastic.
**Rebecca**   How was the weather in Florida?
**Joe**   It was not perfect, but it was ok.
**Rebecca**   Were there any good restaurants?
**Joe**   Yes, there were many good restaurants near the hotel.
**Rebecca**   What was the hotel like?
**Joe**   It was excellent. There was a swimming pool and a tennis court.

### Comprehension Questions!

1. Where did Joe visit?
2. Was the weather perfect?
3. What did the hotel have?

Unit 7 · How was your trip to Florida?

## 1 | Speaking with pictures

With a partner, take turns asking and answering questions about the pictures below.

**A** great, perfect, delicious

**C** exciting, pretty nice, wonderful

**B** terrible, rainy, awful

**A** How was your trip to **Hawaii?**
**B** It was **terrific.**
**A** Was the weather good?
**B** Yes, it was **great.**
**A** How was the food at the hotel?
**B** It was really **awesome.**
**A** You must have **had fun.**

*Check it Out*

## 2 | Speaking some more

Share information about yourself with a partner.

**Your partner** Would you tell me about your last vacation? Where did you go?

**You** I went to _____.

**Your partner** How long were you there?

**You** I was there for _____.

**Your partner** How was the weather?

**You** It was _____.

**Your partner** Who were you with?

**You** _____.

# One Step Ahead!

## 1 Let's talk about you!

**A** Do you remember your first English class? How was it?
**B** Do you remember your first date? How was it?
**C** Do you remember your first overseas holiday? How was it?
**D** Do you remember your first job interview? How was it?

## 2 Let's write about your skills and talents!

Using the grammar points learned in this unit; write about when you were in high school or college.

I CAN!

✓ Talk about my personal history

Unit 8

# What did you do last night?

## 8

### Learning Objectives

After completing this unit, you should be able to...

+ Talk about activities from your recent past

### Getting Started

Answer the questions about the pictures above.

1. Do you sometimes eat snacks late at night?
2. Do you sometimes work at night?
3. What time did you go to bed last night?

Essential English : Begin Again

## Grammatical Expressions

Look at the grammar point below.
Create complete questions with the expressions.
Share your questions and answers with a partner.

**General verb (Past)**

{ I / You / He/She/It / We / They } **got up** early yesterday.

Did { I / You / He/She/It / We / They } **got up** early yesterday?

Yes, ... did.
No, ... didn't.

**Questions with past tense**

What time **did I get up** yesterday?
What **did you do** last night?
Where **did he/she/it go** last night?
How **did we get** to Japan?
Why **did they go** to bed late yesterday?

You **got up** at 7:30 yesterday morning.
I **studied** for a test.
He/She **went** to a party.
We **flew** to Japan.
They went to bed late yesterday because they **watched** a movie.

## Let's Talk

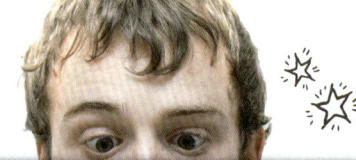
What did you do last night?

Read and practice the conversation with a partner. Then, share your answers to the comprehension questions to check your understanding.

**Steve**   You look tired. What did you do last night?

**Emma**   I studied math. I had a test this morning.

**Steve**   How long did you study?

**Emma**   I studied for about 3 hours. How about you? Did you work late yesterday?

**Steve**   No, I didn't. I went home early and rented a DVD.

**Emma**   Good for you. I'm glad you could relax yesterday.

### Comprehension Questions!

1. What did Emma do last night?
2. Did Steve work late?
3. What did Steve do after work?

Unit 8 · What did you do last night?

## 1 | Speaking with pictures

With a partner, take turns asking and answering questions about the pictures below.

**A** video called a friend
**C** cleaned the house
**B** had a party

- **A** You look tired. What did you do last night?
- **B** I couldn't fall asleep because **I played video games.**
- **A** How long did you **play the game?**
- **B** I **played** for about 3 hours.
- **A** Wow, I never **play video games** for 3 hours.

*Check it Out*

## 2 | Speaking some more

Share information about yourself with a partner.

**Your partner** How much do you remember about yesterday? What did you have for lunch?

**You** I ............................................................................ for lunch.

**Your partner** What time did you go back home?

**You** I ............................................................................ .

**Your partner** What did you do at home at night?

**You** I ............................................................................ .

Essential English : Begin Again

## Grammatical Expressions

Look at the grammar point below.
Create your own sentences using the expressions.
Share your sentences with a partner.

### Past verb form

**Regular**
- visit - visited
- study - studied
- play - played

**Irregular**
- go - went
- get - got
- make - made
- take - took
- have - had
- bring - brought

### Possibility
- last night
- last Monday
- last week
- last year
- yesterday morning
- yesterday afternoon
- yesterday evening

## Let's Talk II

### How was your weekend?

Read and practice the conversation with a partner. Then, share your answers to the comprehension questions to check your understanding.

**Harry**  How was your weekend?

**Esther**  It was great. Gina and I went biking in the park.

**Harry**  Oh, really? That must have been fun for you guys.

**Esther**  Yeah, It was really fun. But there were lots of hills. I was very tired. How did you spend last weekend?

**Harry**  I went to my friend's birthday party. There were many old friends.

**Esther**  Did you see your ex-girlfriend there?

**Harry**  Unfortunately, she did not come.

### Comprehension Questions!

1. What did Gina do this weekend?
2. Why was Esther tired?
3. Who did Harry see this weekend?

Unit 8 · **What did you do last night?**

## 1 | Speaking with pictures

With a partner, take turns asking and answering questions about the pictures below.

A a park, have a picnic

C a theater, watch a movie

B a wedding, meet many old friends

A How was your weekend?
B It was pretty good.
A Where did you go?
B I went to **the beach** with my friend.
A Good. What did you do there?
B We **walked along the beach** and talked a lot.
How about you? Did you have a nice weekend?

*Check it Out*

## 2 | Speaking some more

Share information about your weekend with a partner.

**Your partner** Did you have a nice weekend?

**You** ........................................................................................ .

**Your partner** What did you do?

**You** ........................................................................................ .

**Your partner** Do you usually .................................... on the weekend?

**You** ........................................................................................ .

55

# One Step Ahead!

## 1 Let's talk about you!

**A** What do you usually do after work?
**B** What did you do yesterday evening?
**C** How often do you go to the theater to watch a movie?
**D** When was the last time you saw a movie?

## 2 Let's write about your typical day!

Using the grammar points learned in this unit; write about your typical daily routine.

✓ Talk about activities from my recent past

Unit 9

# What are you going to do?

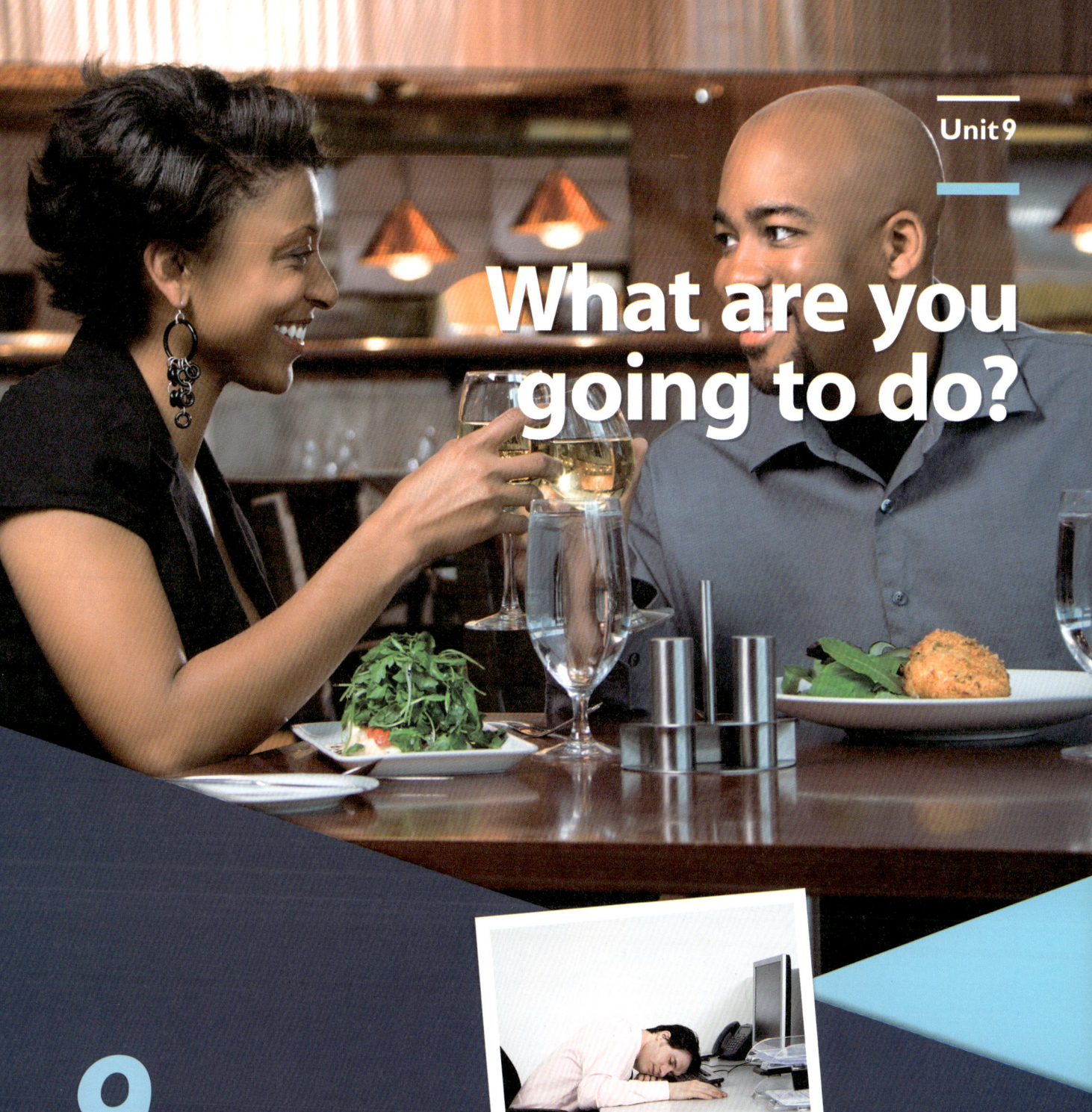

## 9

### Learning Objectives

After completing this unit, you should be able to...

+ Talk about future plans using "going to" and present continuous

### Getting Started

Answer the questions about the pictures above.

1. Are you going to work tonight?
2. Are you going to go out for dinner tonight?
3. What is your best friend going to do today?

Essential English : Begin Again

# Grammatical Expressions

Look at the grammar point below.
Read the sentences and questions.
Create answers to the questions and share them with a partner.

## "going to" for future action

I am going to buy the tickets.
You are going to work tonight.
He/She/It is going to be 29.
We are going to send a card.
They are going to have a party.

Am I going to buy the tickets?
Are you going to work tonight?
Is he/she/it going to be 29?
Are we going to send a card?
Are they going to have a party?

What are you going to do?
What is he/she/it going to do?
What are we/they going to do?

* **Pronunciation Tip :**
  • "going to" is often replaced with "gonna" when speaking.
    "What are we gonna do tonight?"

## Let's Talk 1

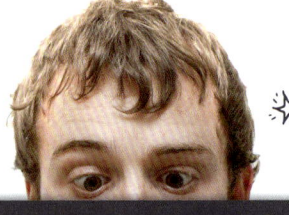

**Read and practice the conversation with a partner. Then, share your answers to the comprehension questions to check your understanding.**

| | |
|---|---|
| **Matthew** | It's mom's birthday this Saturday. She is going to be 50. |
| **Jessica** | That's right. What are you going to get her? |
| **Matthew** | I'm going to buy a necklace for her. |
| **Jessica** | That's a good idea. I am going to get her some flowers. |
| **Matthew** | I am sure she is going to love that. |
| **Jessica** | Where are we going to have the party? |
| **Matthew** | Mom loves that Mexican restaurant downtown. |
| **Jessica** | That will be really nice. |

### Comprehension Questions!

1. How old is Mom going to be?
2. What gifts is she going to receive?
3. Where is the party going to be?

Unit 9 • What are you going to do?

## 1 | Speaking with pictures

With a partner, take turns asking and answering questions about the pictures below.

A buy a coffee maker, get some dishes

C invite our friends, buy some balloons

B buy a car, set him up on a date

A It's Lucy's **birthday** on Saturday.
B What are you going to do for her?
A I am going **to throw a surprise party.**
B That's great. I am going to **get a cake.**
  It will be a great party.

*Check it Out*

## 2 | Speaking some more

Share information about your birthday with a partner.

**Your partner**  It's your birthday today. Are you going to have a party?

**You**  Yes, I ............................................................................ .

**Your partner**  Where are you going to have your party?

**You**  I am going to have my party
................................................................................ .

**Your partner**  What are you going to do at your party?

**You**  I am going to ............................................................ .

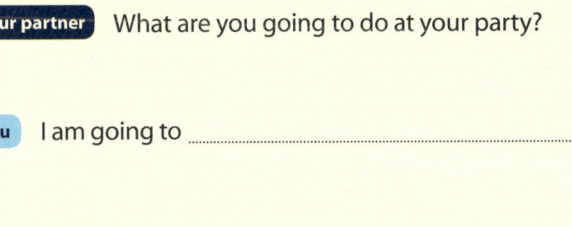

59

Essential English : Begin Again

## Grammatical Expressions

Look at the grammar point below.
Review the questions and create your own answers to each question.
Share your answers with a partner.

### Questions with "be going to"

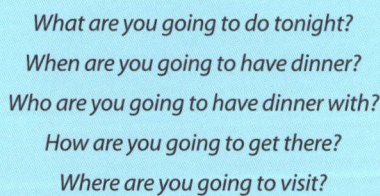

What are you going to do tonight?
When are you going to have dinner?
Who are you going to have dinner with?
How are you going to get there?
Where are you going to visit?

What is he going to do tonight?
When is he going to have dinner?
Who is he going to have dinner with?
How is he going to get there?
Where is he going to visit?

## Let's Talk II

### What are you going to do tonight?

Read and practice the conversation with a partner. Then, share your answers to the comprehension questions to check your understanding.

| | |
|---|---|
| **Jake** | What are you going to do tonight? |
| **Alice** | I'm going to go to a dance party. |
| **Jake** | Me too. Where is the party going to be? |
| **Alice** | It will be at Mary's house. |
| **Jake** | Who are you going to go with? |
| **Alice** | I'm not sure, but I will ask Jason. |
| **Jake** | Jason? Are you sure? |
| | He is going to go with me. |
| **Alice** | Really? I thought he liked me. |

### Comprehension Questions!

1. What is Alice doing tonight?
2. Who is hosting?
3. Who is Jake going with?

Unit 9 · What are you going to do?

## 1 | Speaking with pictures

With a partner, take turns asking and answering questions about the pictures below.

A  Paul, vacation, Florida, Mary

C  Sandy, watch a movie, movie theater, William

B  Kelly, have dinner, restaurant, Tom

- **A** What is **Kevin** going to do on New Year's Eve?
- **B** He is going to **go to a party.**
- **A** Where is the party going to be?
- **B** It will be **at a hotel.**
- **A** Who is he going to go with?
- **B** **He** is going to go with **Sally.**
- **A** Really? I thought **she** liked you.

*Check it Out*

## 2 | Speaking some more

Share information about your plans with a partner.

**Your partner**  Hi, _____ .
Are you doing anything now?

**You**  Yes, _____ .

**Your partner**  Why can't you do that tomorrow?

**You**  Because _____ .

**Your partner**  Oh, I see.

**You**  What _____ ?

61

# One Step Ahead!

## 1. Let's talk about you!

**A** What are you going to do for winter vacation?
**B** What are you going to do on your birthday?
**C** What are you going to do for dinner?

## 2. Let's write about your plans this year!

Using the grammar points learned in this unit; write about what you are going to do before the end of the year.

# I CAN!

✓ Talk about future plans using "going to" and present continuous

Unit 10

# Would you like to go out for dinner?

## 10

### Learning Objectives

After completing this unit, you should be able to...

+ Make an invitation
+ Politely accept or decline invitations

### Getting Started

Answer the questions about the pictures above.

1. How often do you ask your friends to go to the movies?
2. Who would you most like to see in concert?
3. Who would you most like to invite to a party?

Essential English : Begin Again

# Grammatical Expressions

Look at the grammar point below.
Review the invitations and the responses.
Practice the grammar point with a partner.

### Expressions for future invitations

**How to invite**
Are you doing anything tonight?
What are you doing tonight?
Would you like to go out for dinner tonight?
How about dinner with me tonight?

**How to accept**
That's great.
That sounds good.
That's terrific.
That's a good idea.

## Let's Talk I

Would you like to come with me?

Read and practice the conversation with a partner. Then, share your answers to the comprehension questions to check your understanding.

| | |
|---|---|
| Susan | Hello? |
| Mike | Hi, Susan. It's me, Mike. |
| Susan | Hi, Mike. How are you doing? |
| Mike | Not bad. Are you doing anything Saturday night? |
| Susan | Nothing special. Why? |
| Mike | I am going to see a movie. Would you like to come with me? |
| Susan | That's great. What movie are you going to see? |
| Mike | How about Tom Cruise's new film? |

## Comprehension Questions!

1. What night are Mike and Susan going out?
2. What are they going to do?
3. Who stars in the movie?

64

Unit 10 · Would you like to go out for dinner?

## 1 | Speaking with pictures

With a partner, take turns asking and answering questions about the pictures below.

**A** after school, eat pizza, Pizza Inn

**C** tonight, visit a gallery, Art Museum

**B** this weekend, go for a drive, along Ocean View Road

**A** Hi, Connie. What are you going to do **after work?**
**B** Nothing special. Why?
**A** I'm going to **have a drink.** Would you like to come with me?
**B** That sounds good. Where are you going to **have a drink?**
**A** How about **the new restaurant** across from the office?

*Check it Out*

## 2 | Speaking some more

Share information about your plans with a partner.

**Your partner**  Are you _____ tonight?

**You**  Nothing special. Why?

**Your partner**  I'm going to _____ .
Would you like to come?

**You**  That sounds wonderful. I would really love it.

**Your partner**  Where are we going to meet?

**You**  How about _____ ?

65

Essential English : Begin Again

## Grammatical Expressions

Look at the grammar point below.
Review the invitation and the responses.
Practice the grammar point with a partner.

### Expressions for future invitations

**How to invite**

Would you like to have dinner together?

**How to turn down politely**

I'm afraid I can't. I have to take care of my kids.
I'm sorry but I can't. I have to work tonight.
I'd really like to but I can't. Maybe some other time.

## Let's Talk II

### I have to make some food for a Christmas party.

Read and practice the conversation with a partner. Then, share your answers to the comprehension questions to check your understanding.

| | |
|---|---|
| **Ben** | What are you doing Christmas Eve? |
| **Nancy** | Well, I don't know yet. Are you doing something? |
| **Ben** | Yes. I am going to go to a baseball game. |
| **Nancy** | A baseball game on Christmas Eve? |
| **Ben** | Would you like to come with me? |
| **Nancy** | I'm sorry but I can't. I have to make some food for a Christmas party. |
| **Ben** | That's too bad. |
| **Nancy** | Yeah. Maybe some other time. |

### Comprehension Questions!

1. What is Ben doing on Christmas Eve?
2. Why can't Nancy come?

Unit 10 · **Would you like to go out for dinner?**

## 1 | Speaking with pictures

With a partner, take turns asking and answering questions about the pictures below.

A go fishing, study for a test

B go on a picnic, go to a wedding

C go swimming, help my mother

**A** What are you going to do this weekend?

**B** Well, I don't know yet. Are you doing something?

**A** Yes. I am **going to an amusement park.** Would you like to come with me?

**B** I'm afraid I can't. I have to **clean my house.**

**A** Really? Maybe some other time.

*Check it Out*

## 2 | Speaking some more

Share information about your plans with a partner.

**Your partner** What ................................................ this holiday?

**You** Well, I don't know yet. Are ................................................ ?

**Your partner** I am going to ................................................ .
Would you ................................................ ?

**You** I'd really like to, but I can't. I have to ................................................ .

**Your partner** That's too bad. Maybe we can do it next time.

# One Step Ahead!

## 1 Let's talk about you!

A. What is your favorite activity to do after work?
B. What are you going to do tonight?
C. Do you have any plans for this weekend?
D. What do you really want to do during summer vacation?

## 2 Let's write about your plans this year!

Using the grammar points learned in this unit; write about your experience of turning down someone's invitation.

# I CAN!

✓ Make an invitation
✓ Politely accept or decline invitations

# Unit 11

## He's very attractive.

Peter

Ann • Sally • Gary

# 11

## Learning Objectives

After completing this unit, you should be able to...

+ Discuss physical appearances
+ Talk about preferences and attraction

## Getting Started

Answer the questions about the pictures above.

1. Who do you think is thin?
2. Who do you think is attractive?
3. Who do you think is tall?

Essential English : Begin Again

## Grammatical Expressions

Look at the grammar point below.
Review the questions and the answers.
Create your own answers for each question and share them with a partner.

### Adjectives for appearance

I am short.
You are thin.
He is old.
She has long hair.
They have dark hair.

Am I tall?
Are you heavy?
Is he young?
Does she have short hair?
Do they have blond hair?

## Let's Talk

### She is kind of cute.

Read and practice the conversation with a partner. Then, share your answers to the comprehension questions to check your understanding.

| | |
|---|---|
| **Aaron** | So, is your new roommate here? |
| **Joanna** | Yeah, she is right over there. |
| **Aaron** | Does she have short hair? |
| **Joanna** | No, she has long blond hair. |
| **Aaron** | Is she thin and tall? |
| **Joanna** | She is not thin, but she is pretty tall. |
| **Aaron** | Oh, I see. She's the woman with the yellow pants? She's pretty. |
| **Joanna** | Yes, she is kind of cute. |

### Comprehension Questions!

1. What color is Joanna's roommate's hair?
2. Is she tall?
3. What color are her pants?

Unit 11 · He's very attractive.

## 1 | Speaking with pictures

With a partner, take turns asking and answering questions about the pictures below.

A  girlfriend, a ponytail, short

C  fiancée, pierced ears, tall

B  boyfriend, curly hair, thin

A  Is your **brother** here?
B  Yeah, he is right over there.
A  Does **he have a beard**?
B  No, **he** doesn't. **He is bald.**
A  Hmm, is he **muscular**?
B  No, he is not. He is kind of **thin**.

*Check it Out*

## 2 | Speaking some more

Share information about yourself with a partner.

**Your partner**  Is your ................................................ here?

**You**  Yes, ................................................ right over there.

**Your partner**  Does ................ have ................ hair?

**You**  ................................................ .

**Your partner**  Is ................................................ ?

**You**  ................................................ .
She/He is kind of ................................................ .

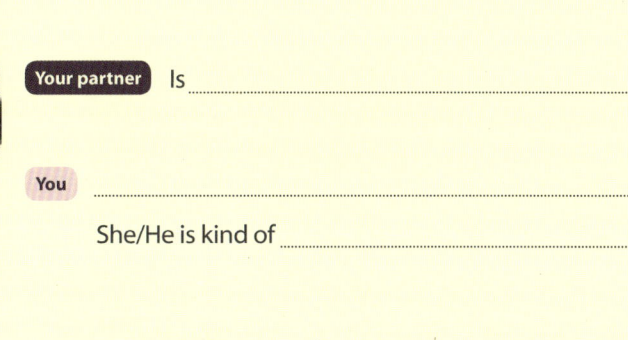

71

Essential English : Begin Again

## Grammatical Expressions

Look at the grammar point below.
Review the questions and the answers.
Create your own answers for each question and share them with a partner.

### Adjectives for appearance

| | |
|---|---|
| What does he look like? | He is tall and good looking. |
| Who does she look like? | She looks like her mother. |
| How tall is she? | She is very tall, about 170 centimeters. |
| What color is her hair? | It's black. |
| How heavy is he? | He is thin. |

## Let's Talk II

### He has curly brown hair.

Read and practice the conversation with a partner. Then, share your answers to the comprehension questions to check your understanding.

**Alex**  Hi, this just arrived for Mr. Kim.
Would you please give this package to him?

**Bianca**  I'm sorry, but I'm new here.
What does he look like?

**Alex**  He is tall and kind of thin.

**Bianca**  What color is his hair?

**Alex**  He has curly brown hair.

**Bianca**  Oh, I know him. I will give it to him.

**Alex**  Thanks a lot.

### Comprehension Questions!

1. Whose package just arrived?
2. What does he look like?
3. Does he have black hair?

Unit 11 · He's very attractive.

## 1 | Speaking with pictures

With a partner, take turns asking and answering questions about the pictures below.

A skinny, model

C cute, pop star

B athletic, sports star

- **A** What does your friend look like?
- **B** He **is kind of** good looking.
- **A** Oh, yeah? How **tall is he?**
- **B** **He** is not short. He is about 177 centimeters.
- **A** Who does he look like?
- **B** **He looks like an actor.**

## Check it Out

## 2 | Speaking some more

Share information about your friends with a partner.

**Your partner** What does your _____ look like?

**You** _____.

**Your partner** How tall is she/he?

**You** _____.

**Your partner** Who does she/he look like?

**You** _____.

# One Step Ahead!

## 1 Let's talk about you!

- **A** Do you like your appearance?
- **B** Do you ever think about plastic surgery?
- **C** What would you like to change about your appearance?
- **D** What kind of person do you find attractive?

## 2 Let's describe your family members!

Using the grammar points learned in this unit; describe yourself and your family members.

# I CAN!

✓ Discuss physical appearances
✓ Talk about preferences and attraction

Unit 12

# It is fantastic.

## 12

### Learning Objectives

**After completing this unit, you should be able to...**

+ Describe personalities
+ Talk about your feelings

### Getting Started

**Answer the questions about the pictures above.**

1. How do you feel before a test?
2. How do you feel when you watch a soccer game?
3. How do you feel when you give a presentation?

Essential English : Begin Again

# Grammatical Expressions

Look at the grammar point below.
Review the questions and the answers.
Create your own answers for each question and share them with a partner.

### Adjectives for personality

| | | | |
|---|---|---|---|
| I am nice. | Am I easygoing? | Yes, you are. | No, you are not. |
| You are friendly. | Are you strict? | Yes, I am. | No, I am not. |
| He is shy. | Is he outgoing? | Yes, he is. | No, he is not. |
| We are quiet. | Are we talkative? | Yes, you are. | No, you are not. |
| They are patient. | Are they impatient? | Yes, they are. | No, they are not. |

## Let's Talk I

### It was awful.

Read and practice the conversation with a partner. Then, share your answers to the comprehension questions to check your understanding.

**John**    Hi, Jessica. How was your date yesterday?

**Jessica**    It was awful. I don't want to think about it.

**John**    What was wrong? What was the man like?

**Jessica**    First, he was 30 minutes late.

**John**    Oh, wow. You must have been really upset.

**Jessica**    And, he was kind of shy and quiet.
He didn't talk much.

**John**    He was very different from your ideal guy.
You like an outgoing and talkative man.

**Jessica**    Yeah. Now I feel really terrible.
So, would you like to buy some ice cream for me?

### Comprehension Questions!

1. How late was Jessica's date?
2. Did he have a friendly personality?
3. What is Jessica's ideal type of guy?

Unit 12 · **It is fantastic.**

## 1 | Speaking with pictures

With a partner, take turns asking and answering questions about the pictures below.

**A** strict, serious, nice

**B** easygoing, patient, friendly

**C** nice, talkative, fun

**A** What is your new **roommate** like?
**B** He **is very friendly.**
**A** Is he **fun**?
**B** Well, not really. But he is **outgoing.**
**A** Oh, that's **good.**

## *Check it Out*

## 2 | Speaking some more

Share information about your best friend with a partner.

**Your partner** Who is your best friend?

**You** My best friend is ............................................. .

**Your partner** What is he/she like?

**You** He/She is ............................................. .

**Your partner** Is he/she ............................................. ?

**You** Yes/No, ............................................. .

**Your partner** Are you two similar or different?

**You** I think we are ............................................. .

77

Essential English : Begin Again

## Grammatical Expressions

Look at the grammar point below.
Read the sentences given in the box.
Use the expressions to share your feelings with a partner.

### Adjectives for feeling

| | |
|---|---|
| I am tired. | My job is tiring. |
| You are worried. | The test is worrying. |
| He is bored. | The movie is boring. |
| She is relaxed. | Classical music is relaxing. |
| We are excited. | The game is exciting. |
| They are interested. | The lesson is interesting. |

## Let's Talk II

### You have to know life is not easy.

Read and practice the conversation with a partner. Then, share your answers to the comprehension questions to check your understanding.

**Tony** How is your new job?

**Alexis** It is hard work. I am so tired.

**Tony** You know, life is not easy.

**Alexis** How about yours?

**Tony** Oh, I like my job a lot. It is exciting.

**Alexis** Good for you. My job is not very interesting.

**Tony** Hey, take your time. You will become interested.

**Alexis** I hope so. Anyway, thanks for cheering me up.

### Comprehension Questions!

1. Is Alexis' job easy?
2. What is Tony's job like?

Unit 12 · It is fantastic.

## 1 | Speaking with pictures

With a partner, take turns asking and answering questions about the pictures below.

A  first day at English class
B  first year in college
C  first day at work

**A** How is your **dance class**?
**B** It is **fantastic.** I am so **interested.**
**A** What is it like?
**B** It is really **exciting and fun.**
**A** That's great.

*Check it Out*

## 2 | Speaking some more

Share information about yourself with a partner.

**Your partner**  How is your new English class?

**You**  It is _____ .
         I am _____ .

**Your partner**  What is it like?

**You**  It is _____ .

**Your partner**  What about your classmates?
         Are they _____ ?

**You**  _____ .

# One Step Ahead!

## 1 Let's talk about you!

A. What kind of person are you? Are you outgoing or shy?
B. What kind of person is your girlfriend/boyfriend/wife/husband?
C. Do you like your personality? If you could change your personality, what would you like to change?

## 2 Let's write about a job interview experience!

Using the grammar points learned in this unit; describe how you felt in a job interview.

_____
_____
_____
_____
_____
_____
_____
_____

# I CAN!

✓ Describe personalities    ✓ Talk about my feelings

Unit 13

# I think I am lost.

## 13

### Learning Objectives

After completing this unit, you should be able to...

+ Use prepositions to describe locations and give directions

### Getting Started

Answer the questions about the pictures above.

1. Is there a café near your office?
2. Is there a supermarket near your home?
3. Is there a bank near your home?

Essential English : Begin Again

## Grammatical Expressions

Look at the grammar point below.
Review the questions and the answers.
Create your own answers for each question and share them with a partner.

### Prepositions for Locations

Is there an internet café near here?
Are there any ATMs near here?

- There is one **behind** the bank.
- It is **in front of** the post office.
- There is one **next to** the bar.
- It is **between** the bank and the post office.
- There are a few **inside** the supermarket.
- There is one **outside** the bank.
- It is **on the corner of** Main and First street.
- There are some **across from** the department store.

\* **ATM** : Automated Teller Machine (cash machine)

## Let's Talk I

### Is there an Internet café near here?

Read and practice the conversation with a partner. Then, share your answers to the comprehension questions to check your understanding.

**Luke**  Excuse me, please. Is there an Internet café near here?

**Ashley**  Uh… there is one on Main Street across from the big department store. It's right up this street.

**Luke**  Thanks. Oh, and are there any cash machines around here?

**Ashley**  Let me see. Yeah. There are some ATMs over there outside the bank, just behind here.

**Luke**  Oh, I see. Thank you so much.

**Ashley**  You're welcome.

### Comprehension Questions!

1. Where is the internet cafe?
2. What else is Luke looking for?
3. Where will he find it?

Unit 13 · I think I am lost.

## 1 | Speaking with pictures

With a partner, take turns asking and answering questions about the map below.

**A** Is there a bank around here?

**B** Yes, there is one right ................................ Main Street.

It's ................................ the deli. Do you see Sam's Deli,

just ................................ the street?

**A** Oh, yeah. Is there a parking lot?

**B** Well, there's one just ................................ the bank.

**A** Are there any public restrooms there?

**B** No, there aren't any. But there's a department store

................................ Main and Third. I'm sure there are

some in the store.

**A** Thanks, and one more thing.

Are there any supermarkets around here?

**B** Uh, there is one over there ................................ the bank.

**A** Thank you so much.

**B** It's my pleasure.

## 2 | Speaking some more

Share information about your surroundings with a partner.

**Your partner** Is there ................................ around here?

**You** Yes, there is one ................................ .

**Your partner** Thank you.

**You** You're welcome.

Essential English : Begin Again

## Grammatical Expressions

Look at the grammar point below.
Read the sentences given in the box.
Use the expressions to share your feelings with a partner.

### Asking and Giving Directions

Could you give me directions to the H hotel?
Can you tell me how to get to City Hall?

- Go straight ahead for two blocks.
- Go down the street about a block.
- Go down/up the stairs.
- Make a right/left turn.
- Turn right/left at the corner

## Let's Talk II

### Excuse me. I think I am lost.

**Read and practice the conversation with a partner. Then, share your answers to the comprehension questions to check your understanding.**

| | |
|---|---|
| **Jeff** | Excuse me. I think I am lost. |
| **Diane** | Where are you headed? |
| **Jeff** | I'm trying to get to the Star Mall. |
| **Diane** | Go straight ahead for three blocks. You're going to see a park. |
| **Jeff** | Three blocks and there is a park. Right? |
| **Diane** | Yes. And then make a right and walk up one block. |
| **Jeff** | Turn right and go one more block. |
| **Diane** | That's right. It's on the left. |
| **Jeff** | Thanks a million. You have been great help. |
| **Diane** | It's my pleasure. |

### Comprehension Questions!

1. Where is Jeff try to go?
2. How far away is the park?
3. What should he do when he sees the park?

Unit 13 · I think I am lost.

## 1 | Speaking with pictures

With a partner, take turns asking and answering questions about the picture below.

**A** Excuse me, I think I am lost.
**B** How can I help you?
**A** Could you give me directions to the Chinese Restaurant?
**B** It is on Charles Street. Just go up one block and turn left. It is on your right.
**A** Go straight one block and make a left turn.
**B** That's right. It's next to the movie theater.
**A** Thanks.
**B** You're welcome.

**A** You are looking for a bookstore.
**B** You are looking for a supermarket.

*Check it Out*

## 2 | Speaking some more

Share information about your surroundings with a partner.

**Your partner** Excuse me. I'm new here. Could you give me directions to the _____ ?

**You** First, you have to _____ .

**Your partner** OK. I have to _____ .

**You** And then you are going to _____ .

**Your partner** Oh, I see.

**You** It is _____ .

# One Step Ahead!

## 1 Let's talk about you!

A. Are you good at reading maps?
B. What do you usually do when you are lost in an unfamiliar place?
C. Do you ever give directions to people who ask for help?

## 2 Let's write about directions!

Using the grammar points learned in this unit; give directions to a café and bank closest to your home.

### I CAN!
✓ Use prepositions to describe locations and give directions

Unit 14

# Would you care for some dessert?

## 14

### Learning Objectives

**After completing this unit, you should be able to...**

+ Accurately use uncountable nouns
+ Use "some" and "any" when offering things to others

### Getting Started

**Answer the questions about the pictures above.**

1. How many cups of coffee do you drink a day?
2. How much fruit do you eat a day?
3. How many hours do you usually sleep?

Essential English : Begin Again

# Grammatical Expressions

Look at the grammar point below.
Review the difference between countable and uncountable nouns.
Practice each expression with a partner.

### Quantifiers

| Countable nouns | Uncountable nouns |
|---|---|
| I have <u>an egg.</u> | I drink <u>milk.</u> |
| I have <u>a few eggs.</u> | I drink <u>a little milk.</u> |
| I have <u>some eggs.</u> | I drink <u>some milk.</u> |
| I have <u>a lot of (many) eggs.</u> | I drink <u>a lot of (much) milk.</u> |
| I don't have <u>many eggs.</u> | I don't drink <u>much milk.</u> |
| Do you have <u>any eggs?</u> | Do you have <u>any milk?</u> |
| I don't have <u>any eggs.</u> | I don't drink <u>any milk.</u> |

## Let's Talk I

### What do you want for dinner?

Read and practice the conversation with a partner. Then, share your answers to the comprehension questions to check your understanding.

**Chris**    What do you want for dinner tonight, honey?

**Belinda**    We eat out all the time. Tonight I'd like to have some fruit, sandwiches, and juice at home.

**Chris**    OK. What do we have in the refrigerator?

**Belinda**    Let's see. We have some carrots but there aren't any apples.

**Chris**    Are there any oranges?

**Belinda**    No, there isn't any fruit. There is only a little milk.

**Chris**    Hum. I have another idea. Let's just go out for dinner.

## Comprehension Questions!

1. What does Belinda want to eat?
2. What is in the refrigerator?
3. What are they going to do for dinner?

Unit 14 · **Would you care for some dessert?**

## 1 | Speaking with pictures

With a partner, take turns asking and answering questions about the pictures below.

A potatoes, cheese
C cucumbers, ice cream
B apples, soda

**A** Are there **any eggs?**
**B** No, there **aren't any eggs.**
**A** Do we have **any bread?**
**B** Yes, we have **a little.**

## 2 | Speaking some more

Share information about making sandwiches with a partner.

**Your partner** What do I need to make a sandwich?

**You** First, you need a lot of _____ and some _____ .

**Your partner** Do I need any _____ ?

**You** Maybe/Maybe not. I think you also need a little _____ and a few _____ .

**Your partner** Thanks for helping me. You are a good cook.

**You** I love cooking, but I am not a good cook.

89

Essential English : Begin Again

## Grammatical Expressions

Look at the grammar point below.
Review the difference between using 'some' and 'any'.
Practice each expression with a partner.

### Some and Any

Use *some* when we request and offer things.

Would you like some cookies?
Would you like something to drink?

Use *any* when we ask a question to get information.

Is there any tea in the jar?
Are there any cookies in the jar?
Do you have any brothers or sisters?
Is there anything you want to buy?

## Let's Talk II

### I am watching my weight.

Read and practice the conversation with a partner. Then, share your answers to the comprehension questions to check your understanding.

| | |
|---|---|
| **Josh** | Thanks for inviting me for dinner. |
| **Hillary** | Oh, it's my pleasure. Would you like a drink? |
| **Josh** | Thanks. I'd like to have some chocolate milk. |
| **Hillary** | Would you care for some dessert? |
| **Josh** | Do you have any sweets? |
| **Hillary** | Of course. There are a lot of cookies. I made them by myself. Help yourself. |
| **Josh** | Oh, these are wonderful. But my doctor says I should watch my weight and only eat a few cookies. |
| **Hillary** | Don't worry. You look okay. |

### Comprehension Questions!

1. What would Josh like to drink?
2. Who made the cookies?
3. Can Josh eat a lot of cookies? Why or why not?

## 1 | Speaking with pictures

With a partner, take turns asking and answering questions about the pictures below.

A cake, coffee
C fruit, lemonade
B donuts, milk

**A** Would you like some **candy?**

**B** Oh, I'd love some, but I am on a diet.

**A** Don't worry. You look okay.

**B** Well, then I will take just **a few candies.**

**A** Would you care for some **tea?**

**B** Oh, that's great. I think it is okay to drink **a lot of tea.**

*Check it Out*

## 2 | Speaking some more

Share information about yourself with a partner.

**Your partner**  Would you like some ..................................................?

**You**  Oh, no thanks. I am on a diet.

**Your partner**  Don't be silly. You look ................................................. .

**You**  Let me have just a bite.

**Your partner**  Would you care for some ................................................., too?

**You**  Oh, that's my favorite.

# One Step Ahead!

### 1  Let's talk about you!

- **A** How often do you eat out?
- **B** What kind of food do you like?
- **C** Do you usually eat desserts?

### 2  Let's write about your favorite food and restaurants!

Using the grammar points learned in this unit; write about your favorite food and restaurant.

# I CAN!

✓ Accurately use uncountable nouns

✓ Use "some" and "any" when offering things to others

Unit 15

# Do you mind if I use your car?

## 15

### Learning Objectives

**After completing this unit, you should be able to...**

+ Accurately use modal verbs to offer or request help
+ Politely ask for permission and respond to requests

### Getting Started

**Answer the questions about the picture above.**

1. What is the man saying?
2. What is the girl saying?
3. Do you ever ask for favors from your friends?

## Grammatical Expressions

Look at the grammar point below. Review the information and create your own questions using the model verbs. Share your questions with a partner.

### Modal Verbs : Offering and Requesting

Offering help
Requesting politely

**May I** help you?
**May I** borrow your laptop?
**Could I** borrow your camera?
**Can I** borrow some money?
**Would you** help me?
**Could you** help me?
**Can you** help me?

## Let's Talk

### Could you tell him to call me later?

Read and practice the conversation with a partner. Then, share your answers to the comprehension questions to check your understanding.

**Emma**    Good morning. May I help you?
**Peter**    Yes, can I speak to Louis Park please?
**Emma**    I'm sorry, but he isn't here at this moment. May I take a message?
**Peter**    Thanks. Could you tell him to call me later? My name is Peter.
**Emma**    Sure, sir. Would you like to leave your number?
**Peter**    Oh, he knows my number. Thanks anyway.
**Emma**    OK. I will give him the message. Have a nice day.

### Comprehension Questions!

1. Who wants to speak with Louis?
2. What message does he leave?
3. Why doesn't he leave his phone number?

Unit 15 · Do you mind if I use your car?

## 1 | Speaking with pictures

With a partner, take turns asking and answering questions about the pictures below.

**A** in a meeting, Kevin from A. Telecommunications

**C** having lunch, Bill from I. Networks

**B** on vacation, Nancy from B. Computers

**A** Hello, this is S. Consulting. May I help you?
**B** Can I speak to Mr. Kim?
**A** Sorry, sir. He is **out** now.
**B** Would you take a message for me?
**A** Sure. May I have your name, please?
**B** This is **James from BG Marketing.** Would you tell him to call me in the afternoon?
**A** Certainly sir.

*Check it Out*

## 2 | Speaking some more

Share information about yourself with a partner.

**Your partner** Hello, this is M. Bank. May I help you?

**You** May I ........................................................................?

**Your partner** I'm sorry, but ........................................................................ .

**You** Could you ........................................................................?

**Your partner** Sure. ........................ your name and phone number?

**You** ........................................................................ .

Essential English : Begin Again

## Grammatical Expressions

Look at the grammar point below.
Review the questions and responses.
Practice each expression with a partner.

### Getting Permission and Responding

May I ask a favor?
Can I use your camera?
Do you mind if I use your dictionary?

Yes, go ahead.
Sure. What is it?
Certainly
I am sorry, but I don't have a camera.
No, not at all.

## Let's Talk II

*Do you mind if I use your car tonight?*

Read and practice the conversation with a partner. Then, share your answers to the comprehension questions to check your understanding.

| | |
|---|---|
| **Sam** | Paul. May I ask you a favor? |
| **Paul** | Sure. How can I help you? |
| **Sam** | Can I borrow your suit tonight? |
| **Paul** | Certainly. What happened to yours? |
| **Sam** | Oh, mine is too dirty. Then one more thing. Do you mind if I use your car tonight? |
| **Paul** | My car? Where are you going tonight? |
| **Sam** | I am going to a dance party with Ann. |
| **Paul** | With Ann? I thought you guys broke up. |

### Comprehension Questions!

1. Who does Sam ask for a favor?
2. What does Sam request?
3. Why does Sam need Paul's help?

Unit 15 · Do you mind if I use your car?

## 1 | Speaking with pictures

With a partner, take turns asking and answering questions about the pictures below.

A go to a movie, stay over at my friend's

C borrow money, borrow a credit card

B go on a picnic, borrow your car

**A** Mom. May **I go out with friends tonight?**
**B** Well, you may.
**A** And do you mind if **I stay out all night dancing?**
**B** Well, I am not sure. I have to think about it.

*Check it Out*

## 2 | Speaking some more

Share information about what favors you need with a partner.

**Your partner**  May I ask a favor?

**You**  Sure. What is it?

**Your partner**  I am so tired now. Could you ........................................?

**You**  Certainly. I can do that.

**Your partner**  One more thing. May I ........................................?

**You**  Well, let me think about it.

# One Step Ahead!

## 1. Let's talk about you!

A. Do you ever borrow money from friends or parents?
B. Do you always pay back that money?
C. If your friend asked to borrow your car, what would you do?

## 2. Let's write about an embarrassing situation!

Using the grammar points learned in this unit; write about what you might do if you accidentally lost something you borrowed from a friend.

## I CAN!

✓ Accurately use modal verbs to offer or request help

✓ Politely ask for permission and respond to requests

Unit 16

# Wasn't it a little scary?

## 16

### Learning Objectives

After completing this unit, you should be able to...

+ Accurately ask and respond to tag questions
+ Accurately ask and respond to negative questions

### Getting Started

Answer the questions about the pictures above.

1. Do you think the man in the small picture is happy?
2. What might the couple be doing?
3. Do you think the couple is happy?

Essential English : Begin Again

## Grammatical Expressions

Look at the grammar point below.
Read the questions and share your responses to the questions with a partner.

### Tag Questions

I'm late, aren't I?
You are hungry, aren't you?
Jessica is visiting England, isn't she?
James worked last Saturday, didn't he?
We have extra time, don't we?
We will have a meeting today, won't we?
They can speak Chinese, can't they?

I'm not late, am I?
You aren't hungry, are you?
Jessica isn't working now, is she?
James didn't work last Saturday, did he?
We don't have extra time, do we?
We won't have a meeting today, will we?
They can't speak Chinese, can they?

## Let's Talk I

### I can't have my lunch, can I?

Read and practice the conversation with a partner. Then, share your answers to the comprehension questions to check your understanding.

**Colin** Maria, let's check my schedule for today. I have a meeting this afternoon, don't I?

**Maria** Yes, that's right. With Henry and Tom.

**Colin** The meeting is here, isn't it?

**Maria** No, it isn't. It's in Tom's office at 3 p.m.

**Colin** OK. And I signed all my papers, didn't I?

**Maria** No, you didn't. They're on your desk, sir.

**Colin** Maria, come on. Can't I have my lunch?

### Comprehension Questions!

1. Who is Colin meeting this afternoon?
2. Where is the meeting?
3. What time is the meeting?

Unit 16 · Wasn't it a little scary?

## 1 | Speaking with pictures

With a partner, take turns asking and answering questions about the pictures below.

**A** Carl. Jane is kind of cute, ................?
**B** Oh, you are interested in her, ................?
**A** A little. She doesn't have a boy friend, ................?
**B** Well, I don't know. Why don't you ask her?

**A** Kevin. It is hot in here, ................?
**B** Yes, a little. This room has an air conditioner, ................?
**A** I guess so. By the way, the meeting will begin at 2:00, ................?
**B** Well, I am not sure. Why don't we ask the HR manager?

*Check it Out*

## 2 | Speaking some more

Share information about yourself with a partner.

**Your partner** You already had lunch with a client, ................?

**You** Yes/No, ................ .

**Your partner** You will have a meeting at 4:00 today, ................?

**You** Yes/No, ................ .

**Your partner** You are taking an English class now, ................?

**You** Yes/No, ................ .

101

Essential English : Begin Again

# Grammatical Expressions

Look at the grammar point below.
Review the questions and responses.
Practice the expressions with a partner.

## Negative Questions

**To check information**

| | |
|---|---|
| Isn't Jane a vegetarian? | Yes, she is. |
| Don't they have two sons? | No, they don't. |

**When you want someone to agree with you**

| | |
|---|---|
| Don't you like Italian food? | Yes, it's delicious. |
| Wasn't that a terrible dinner? | Actually, I disagree. I liked it |

**To express surprise**

| | |
|---|---|
| Weren't you going to bring cake? | Yes, I was. I'm sorry. I forgot. |
| Did you say you don't like meat? | Me? No, I love it. |

# Let's Talk II

## Wasn't it a little scary?

Read and practice the conversation with a partner. Then, share your answers to the comprehension questions to check your understanding.

**Gary**    The movie was great. Don't you think so?

**Elena**    Yes, I do. But wasn't it a little scary?

**Gary**    No, it wasn't at all. By the way, aren't you hungry?

**Elena**    Yes, I am starving. Oh, there is a pizza place over there. Do you want to go there?

**Gary**    I am sorry, but I had pizza for lunch. How about spicy food?

**Elena**    Oh, I don't mind. Isn't there a Mexican Restaurant near here?

**Gary**    Yes, there is. I know where it is. Let's go.

## Comprehension Questions!

1. What does Gary think of the movie?
2. Why doesn't Gary want pizza?
3. What kind of food are they going to eat?

## 1 | Speaking with pictures

With a partner, take turns asking and answering questions about the pictures below.

**A** I love this place. ................ this a nice restaurant?
**B** I think so. But ................ you allergic to seafood?
**A** Me? No. I love seafood. ................ you like seafood?
**B** It is okay for me. Actually I am a vegetarian.
**A** Really? So, ................ you eat any seafood?
**B** Don't worry about it. I will have some salad.

**A** ................ you have a meeting right now?
**B** No, not yet. I will have it after lunch.
**A** Oh, I see. ................ you nervous? I heard this is really important for our company.
**B** Yes, it is. I have to do my best.
**A** By the way, ................ you had lunch yet? If you haven't had lunch yet, let's have it together.
**B** That's a great idea.

## 2 | Speaking some more

Share information about having a job interview with a partner.

**Your partner** ................ you going to have a job interview tomorrow?

**You** Yes/No, ................................................ .

**Your partner** ................ you nervous now?

**You** Yes/No, ................................................ .

**Your partner** ................ you get some information about that company?

**You** Yes/No, ................................................ .

103

# One Step Ahead!

## 1  Let's talk about you!

- **A** You enjoy your work, don't you?
- **B** You are happy now, aren't you?
- **C** Aren't you studying a lot of English these days?
- **D** Don't you like Thai food?

## 2  Let's write about you and your friends!

Using the grammar points learned in this unit; write about yourself and your friends.

## I CAN!

✓ Accurately ask and respond to tag questions

✓ Accurately ask and respond to negative questions